P9-DCJ-190

Bedtime Math²™

THIS TIME IT'S PERSONAL

Laura Overdeck
Illustrated by Jim Paillot

Feiwel and Friends
New York

A Feiwel and Friends Book
An Imprint of Macmillan

Feiwel and Friends books may be purchased for business or promotional use.
For information on bulk purchases, please contact the Macmillan Corporate and
Premium Sales Department at (800) 221-7945 x5442 or by e-mail at
specialmarkets@macmillan.com.

Library of Congress Cataloging-in-Publication Data Available

ISBN: 978-1-250-04096-1 (hardcover) / 978-1-250-05897-3 (ebook)

Book design by Ashley Halsey

Feiwel and Friends logo designed by Filomena Tuosto

First Edition: 2014

10 9 8 7 6 5 4 3 2 1

mackids.com

To John, my beloved husband . . .
this math adventure couldn't have
happened without you.

Introduction

We all know to read to our kids at night, but what about math? Bedtime Math's goal is to make math as common and beloved as the bedtime story.

For many people, that's a tall order. We all know plenty of grown-ups as well as kids who don't like math, who find it tedious and maybe outright nerve-wracking. This fear then becomes a sad self-fulfilling prophecy: Studies using MRIs show that math anxiety blocks working memory, making people score worse on tests regardless of their skills. While there are people who love math from the get-go, overall math has a pretty unpopular image in our culture, and that's what Bedtime Math hopes to change.

We can prevent math anxiety, and in fact reverse it. It all boils down to making math appealing for kids right from the start. If kids like flamingos, frogs, and chocolate chips, then let's give them math problems about flamingos, frogs, and chocolate chips! That's how I started the Bedtime Math Web site, which serves up a zany new math problem every day. This book and its prequel, *Bedtime Math*, take that concept to the next level, with an even wilder variety of topics and lively color illustrations.

In what we at Bedtime Math call the "fun framework," math for kids can't be just tolerable or even engaging if we want to overhaul our culture. Math needs to be compelling—content that kids seek out and enjoy right alongside other favorite activities. Given that math anxiety has been shown to start as early as age five, it's important that we give kids the most enjoyable first impression of math that we can.

It's critical because kids need math skills to become capable adults. Kids love to imagine great inventions that they might create: a car that flies; a bike

that's powered by lightning; a blender that turns broccoli into brownies. Someday our kids will have the chance to become real inventors, and the only way they'll fulfill that dream is if they have math, science, and technological training. And even kids who don't go into such jobs need math skills to get through regular life. One day when your grown child takes out a loan, she or he should be able to estimate the long-term overall cost. Anytime there's a warranty on an offer, she or he should know the chances of breaking that item versus saving the money. Smart day-to-day decisions like figuring out sales discounts, paying the tip at a res-taurant, and knowing that winning the lottery is less likely than becoming an astronaut also require good math skills.

On a more serious level, our quality of life as a society depends on these kids. If we want medicines without bad side effects, cell phones that don't keep dropping calls, or cheap, clean energy, we need a next generation of technologically talented adults—and that requires math. Whether kids want to change other people's lives or just thrive on their own, they will need math skills, and *Bedtime Math* is a great place to start building them.

How to Do Bedtime Math—The Fun Way

Don't sweat it. Choose the level of challenge that works best. There's a reason we don't list a "correct" age range for each problem. The three levels of challenge are labeled "Wee ones," "Little kids," and "Big kids" precisely to avoid specific ages or grade levels. The first level is named "Wee ones" to emphasize that kids should start doing math as preschoolers. The more math at home before kindergarten, the better. With **"Wee ones,"** your child can have fun comparing numbers, finding shapes, and counting objects. **"Little kids"** moves your child on to single-digit adding and subtracting, as well as simple logic puzzles. **"Big kids"** introduces the excitement of wrestling with bigger numbers, as they build on all their little-number learning and discover, for instance, that multiplication is just a speedy way to add. And finally, this book adds a **"Bonus"** level, where readers tackle math acrobatics that require two or more separate steps. All levels, however, are great mental warm-ups for *anyone*, all the way up to the grandparents who use the Web site as a daily brainteaser. So just jump right in, and see what level seems like a comfortable starting point.

It's an activity, not a test. The goal is to have an entertaining conversation that leads to the answer, not to see if your kids can get the answer right off the bat. Read the math problem aloud, then walk through the steps to solve it, and please feel free to give hints when needed. For more pointers, you can also check out the Equation Chart at the back of the book—a.k.a. the math behind the fun.

Don't worry about your kids getting wound up. We haven't seen that happen with Bedtime Math. After all, the time-honored way to fall asleep is to count sheep! Numbers are soothing and predictable, and math problems give kids a reason to settle down and focus. Besides, what better way to end the day than by accomplishing something?

Don't sweat it. Part II. Yes, we'd love to become part of your routine every single day. But we all have those days that begin with the roof falling through to the first floor, and we just can't quite get to every wholesome activity. *Bedtime Math*—this book, as well as all the content on the Web site—is here for you when you're ready for it.

Any time of day can work. We do talk about nighttime a lot, but Bedtime Math can become a part of any routine: breakfast, carpool, dinnertime, bath time. If you weave it into a daily activity, it can become a natural habit.

Stretch. Because it's a team effort, you can reach as high as you and your child want to try. There's something

magical about adding two big numbers for the first time ever, or multiplying 5 times 5. While teachers can't have that playful one-on-one with twenty-three students at once, you *can* do this at home, and you'll find that kids love to tackle the tougher challenge levels.

It's beautiful. Again, we never hear people say, "Ewww, a book at bedtime?!" Likewise, there's absolutely no reason to say that about math. Numbers are beautiful, and kids love attention. *Bedtime Math* just puts the two together. With that, let the games begin!

10 8 34 23 4 14 100 25 42 6 13 6

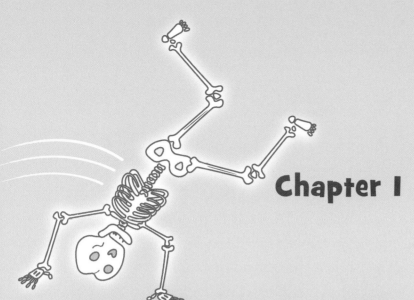

Chapter 1

WHAT'S IN YOU?

133 2 9 11 95 29 8 53 1 22 36 15

Stick People

It's a good thing your body has bones inside it, or you wouldn't be able to sit, stand, or do cartwheels—you'd just collapse to the floor like a melted marshmallow. Thankfully, your body has over 200 bones, and they don't just hold you up. The biggest bone of all is in the top half of your leg, called the femur (which does hold you up). But the teeniest bones in your body—the hammer, anvil, and stirrup inside your ear—actually help you hear. We're lucky that each bone does its own thing, otherwise you might have to walk on your fingers or write with your nose.

💀 **Wee ones:** Each of your fingers has 3 bones, but each toe has only 2. Which one has more bones, your finger or your toe?

💀💀 **Little kids:** You were born without real kneecaps! They start out mushy and don't harden until age 4 or 5. If you have 3 babies and 2 grown-ups in the room, how many "real" kneecaps are there? (Each person has 2 legs, but only some kneecaps count.)

💀💀💀 **Big kids:** Your thumb is actually your longest finger: It has 3 bones like the others, but the third bone is hidden in your hand. How many bones do your 5 fingers on one hand have in total?

⭐ **Bonus:** We're all born with more bones than we end up with, since many bones grow together over time. If you started with 350 bones and now have 206, how many more did you start with?

The Tooth of the Matter

Isn't it kind of weird that when you're a kid, your teeth fall out? You wouldn't be so calm if your nose suddenly popped off, that's for sure. But losing your teeth is normal. Your first set, called baby teeth, has just 20 teeth. They start falling out when you're between 4 and 7 years old, and hopefully not because you had them knocked out by a flying baseball. The good news is, you replace all those baby teeth with a whole new set, up to 32 of them. The bad news is, if those teeth fall out, you won't grow any more!

Wee ones: How many teeth are running away from the girl in the picture? Count them!

Little kids: How many legs do those crazy teeth have altogether?

Big kids: Most mammals—like dogs, rabbits, and beavers—lose their baby teeth, too. If this year you lose 9 teeth, and next year you lose 3 more and your dog loses 7, how many teeth did you lose together?

★ Bonus: Anteaters don't need teeth at all. If there are 38 picnickers at a picnic and half are people and the other half are anteaters, how many picnickers have no teeth?

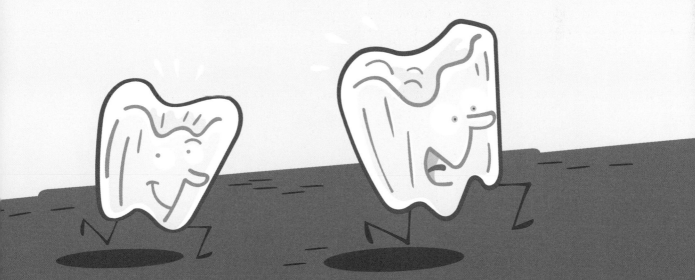

Foot in Your Mouth—or on Your Arm

People come in all shapes and sizes, but some body parts always relate to each other in a certain way. For instance, your foot matches the length from your elbow crease to your wrist, or comes very close. Really! Hold your foot up to your arm, and the length will match. Meanwhile, your head is about 4 to 5 times as wide as your eye, although thankfully we don't all have 4 eyeballs—life would look so confusing. In any case, try measuring your own body parts and see how they all line up.

🦶 **Wee ones:** Which is longer, your hand or your whole arm?

🦶🦶 **Little kids:** If you actually had 5 eyes instead of 2, how many more eyes would you have than you do now?

🦶🦶🦶 **Big kids:** If you stretch your arms to the side, that width is about the same as your height. If your arms span 41 inches and you're just 2 inches taller than that, how tall are you?

⭐ **Bonus:** If you're 7 times as tall as your 7-inch-tall head, how tall are you?

Answers: Your arm; 3 more eyes; 43 inches; 49 inches.

You've Nailed It

If you try to watch your fingernails grow, trust us, it won't be very exciting. Fingernails grow only about 1/10 of an inch per month, which is s-l-o-w. That does add up over time, though, which means we have to clip and file them. Otherwise, they'll grow too long and curl under like the claws on tigers, guinea pigs, and other animals who for whatever reason don't own nail clippers. Our toenails are easier on us, they grow 4 times as slowly as our fingernails . . . and that makes your fingernails look exciting.

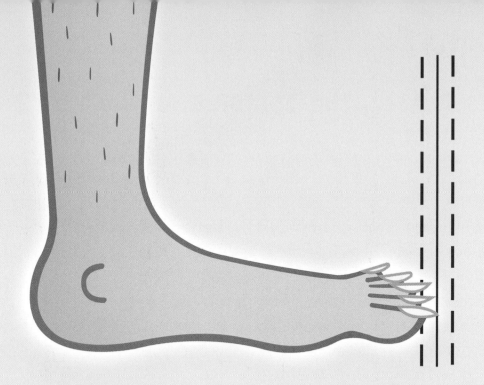

🌙 **Wee ones:** How many fingernails do you have on 1 hand? Count them with a grown-up!

🌙🌙 **Little kids:** If you have 5 fingers on each hand and 5 toes on each foot, how many nails do you have in total?

🌙🌙🌙 **Big kids:** If fingernails take 10 months to grow an inch and toenails take 4 times as long, how fast will your toenail grow an inch?

⭐ **Bonus:** If you've already gone 7 months without clipping your nails, and you decide to go another 3 years to see what happens, for how many months total will you skip nail-clipping?

Who's Faster, the Tortoise or the Hair?

If you thought watching your nails grow was exciting, now you can watch your hair. And you have plenty of it to watch, because you have hair on every single part of your skin except your lips, the tops of your eyelids, the palms of your hands, and the bottoms of your feet. The rest of your body has hair, but most of it is so tiny that you can't see it. Your hair grows very slowly, but at an inch every 2 months, it's a lot faster than those fingernails. Since hair grows faster, you have to cut it more often, but what happens if you just let it go?

Wee ones: If you can spike your hair 6 inches tall on the top of your head, and the kid down the street can spike his hair 4 inches tall, who has the longer, spikier spikes?

Little kids: If you have no hair on your lips, your eyelids, your palms, or the soles of your feet, how many body parts don't have hair? Count them up! (Remember, there are 2 of each part!)

Big kids: If your hair is 26 inches long and you need another 11 inches to reach your ankles, how long will your hair be?

★ **Bonus:** If hair grows 1 inch every 2 months and right now the end of your hair swishes just 28 inches off the floor, how soon can your hair grow to the ground?

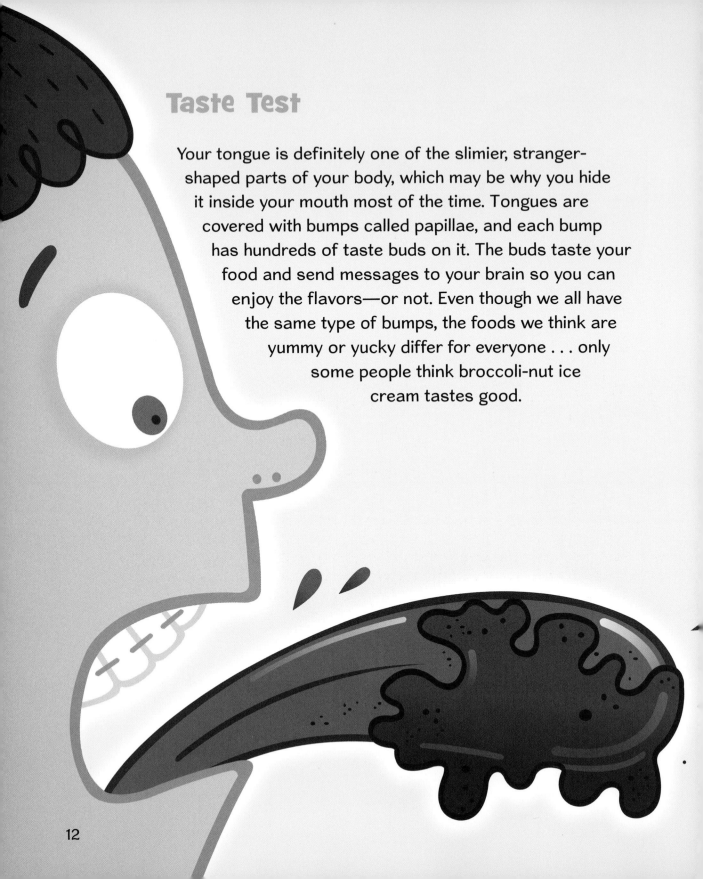

Taste Test

Your tongue is definitely one of the slimier, stranger-shaped parts of your body, which may be why you hide it inside your mouth most of the time. Tongues are covered with bumps called papillae, and each bump has hundreds of taste buds on it. The buds taste your food and send messages to your brain so you can enjoy the flavors—or not. Even though we all have the same type of bumps, the foods we think are yummy or yucky differ for everyone . . . only some people think broccoli-nut ice cream tastes good.

Wee ones: Your tongue can taste 5 basic flavors: sweet, salty, sour, bitter, and umami (basically meat-flavor). But how many "tasty zones" are on the chart here?

Little kids: If you're willing to try 10 weird new foods every week and you have 34 to try, how many new foods are left to try after 3 weeks?

Big kids: They say it can take up to 8 times tasting a new food before you finally like it. If you taste 3 new foods—say kangaroo, kiwi, and shark—up to how many tastes might it take to like them all?

⭐ **Bonus:** Half your taste buds will stop working by the time you're age 20. If you start with 4,600, how many buds will still be working?

I gotta go!

Are We There Yet?

When you're about to go on a long car ride, that is not the best time to drink a gallon of water. A lot of the water you drink gets soaked up by your stomach and intestines, but some of it runs right through you and comes out your other end as pee. How long that takes depends on how much you drank, how hot it is outside, and how long ago you ate, among other things. But water could take an hour or less to go through you, so make sure there's a potty stop on the trip.

Again?

💧 **Wee ones:** What shape is the sleeping boy's window?

💧💧 **Little kids:** If you think you'll need to pee in 10 minutes, but the next rest stop is 12 minutes away, for how much extra time will you have to hold it in?

💧💧💧 **Big kids:** If you drink 22 ounces of water and your body pees all but 9 ounces of it, how much of it comes out as pee?

⭐ **Bonus:** If you'll need to pee in 45 minutes and it's now 3:28 p.m., at what time will you need a potty stop?

Getting Loud

Each of us has our own voice, different from everyone else's. Even when you sing low or make a high squeak, you still basically sound like you. So what's causing all that noise? Your windpipe has vocal chords stretched across it, and when you talk, they close shut so the air has to blow through them. This makes them shake, as if you'd plucked a guitar, and they make a sound. To give a sense of how loud you are, you whisper at about 15 decibels and talk at about 60 decibels, but if you want to yell as loud as a 120-decibel jet engine, you'll have to practice.

♪ **Wee ones:** If you whisper 1! really quietly, then 2, 3, 4, and 5, what number do you whisper next?

♪♪ **Little kids:** If you and 6 friends are talking during the movie and 3 of you shush like you should, how many of you still need to quiet down?

♪♪♪ **Big kids:** The musical notes of a scale are A, B, C, D, E, F, G, and then they start over at A. If you sing a low A, then trill the note 10 notes higher like an opera singer, what note do you sing?

★ **Bonus:** If you can yell at 75 decibels, but your very loud best friend can shriek at 92 decibels, how many decibels louder is your friend?

Answers: 6; 4 of you (since there are 7 in total); a high D; 17 decibels louder.

29 31 60 45 10 6 17 69 26 4 15

Chapter 2

WHAT'S ON YOU?

Under Where?

Underwear is that strange piece of clothing no one sees on us, but we still care what it looks like. We don't want to wear underwear that's goofy shaped, full of holes, or decorated with a cartoon character we haven't liked in 3 years. That's why things turn desperate when the laundry hasn't been washed in a few days and we run out of underwear. How many pairs do we need to get through the week—and if we run out, how many people are we willing to tell?

Wee ones: If you go back and forth between striped underwear and purple-elephant underwear, and you wore stripes yesterday and elephants today, which kind will you wear tomorrow?

Little kids: If the kids in your house have a total of 9 superhero pairs of underwear and 4 peace-sign pairs, how many total pairs do you all have?

Big kids: If you have 30 pairs of underwear—3 neon, 8 polka-dots, and the rest plain old white—how many white pairs do you have?

Bonus: If you have 7 pairs of underwear that you always wear in the same order, how many pairs will you get to wear 5 times in a 30-day month instead of just 4 times?

An Eye for an Eye

Glasses and goggles are the only things that sit right in front of our eyes but help us see. Lots of people wear glasses all day, but eyewear gets way more interesting than that. Sunglasses help you see in the bright sun without squinting. Water goggles let you see underwater without the water coming right up to your eyeballs. The best glasses of all might be night-vision goggles, which see heat instead of light and help you spot night critters as far as 50 or 70 feet away. It just goes to show that 4 eyes are definitely better than 2.

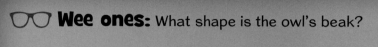 **Wee ones:** What shape is the owl's beak?

Little kids: If you're playing night-vision hide-and-seek and you count to 100 by 10s, what numbers do you call out before "Ready or not, here I come!"?

Big kids: If your night-vision goggles let you see for 51 feet and there's a deer standing 72 feet from you, how many more feet do you have to sneak up to see it?

★ **Bonus:** Some people wear contact lenses: clear mini-circles that stick to your eyeball. If you wear 1 new pair a day, how many lenses do you wear in a year? (Use a 365-day year.)

Socks on the Run

Why don't socks have snaps so we can stick them together before tossing them in the wash? Of all your pairs of socks, chances are at least 2 have gone missing, and of course they probably aren't from the same pair. You can try wearing a sock from one pair and a sock from another, but if one has stripes and the other has polka dots, it's going to be obvious you messed up. Maybe we should all just agree to wear whatever two socks we grab first, whether they match or not.

L Wee ones: How many socks do you see in the row of feet?

LL Little kid: If you own 10 pairs of socks and you've matched up 6 pairs so far, how many more pairs do you still need to track down?

LLL Big kids: If you have 17 socks in the drawer, but there are only 6 matching pairs, how many extra socks do you have left to make sock puppets?

⭐ **Bonus:** If you have 4 loose pairs of socks in the drawer (red, green, blue, and white) and you grab 2 loose socks without looking, how many different color combos could you grab?

Answers: 10 socks; 4 more pairs; 5 socks (since 12 are matched); 10 kinds of pairs (the 4 matching pairs, plus RG, RB, RW, GB, GW, and BW).

Mess Magnet

What you have on you and what you're supposed to have on you are sometimes very different things. You're supposed to be wearing clothes or at least a swimsuit, but by day's end you're probably also wearing mud, sand, chocolate sauce, and other junk. Dry stuff like dust or powdered sugar might brush off easily, but if you get into mud or wet sand, things get sticky fast. A little trick: If you rub talcum powder onto wet sand stuck to you, it won't stick anymore—it will magically fall off. On the other hand, if you like being a mess, then don't bother.

⭐ **Wee ones:** If you run around at a picnic and come home covered with mud, sand, and ketchup, how many kinds of mess are you wearing?

⭐⭐ **Little kids:** If you're baking and you somehow get 7 tablespoons of flour on your shirt but your friend gets 11 tablespoons of flour in her hair, who's covered with more mess?

⭐⭐⭐ **Big kids:** Pigs and other animals roll in the mud on purpose to cool off. If it's 80 degrees out and you roll around in nice 60-degree mud, how much cooler is that mud?

⭐ **Bonus:** If you have 200 grains of sand stuck to your feet and twice as many grains on each leg, how much sand is stuck to you?

Answers: 3 messy things; your friend; 20 degrees; 1,000 grains (including 400 on each leg).

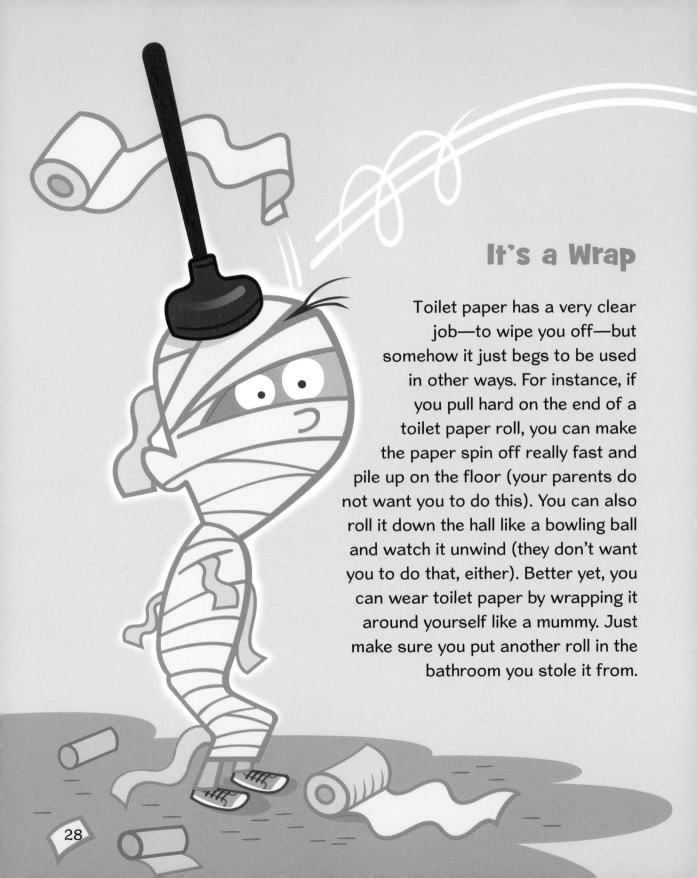

It's a Wrap

Toilet paper has a very clear job—to wipe you off—but somehow it just begs to be used in other ways. For instance, if you pull hard on the end of a toilet paper roll, you can make the paper spin off really fast and pile up on the floor (your parents do not want you to do this). You can also roll it down the hall like a bowling ball and watch it unwind (they don't want you to do that, either). Better yet, you can wear toilet paper by wrapping it around yourself like a mummy. Just make sure you put another roll in the bathroom you stole it from.

Wee ones: Which is longer, a 4-square piece of toilet paper or a 2-square piece?

Little kids: If you're yanking the toilet paper and counting the squares that roll off and you've counted to 13, what are the next 4 numbers you count?

Big kids: If you throw a roll of toilet paper and it unrolls 53 squares, then bounces and unrolls another 10 squares, how many squares did you unroll?

★ Bonus: Toilet paper squares are usually 4 inches long (and wide). If you wrap 96 squares around you, how many feet of toilet paper is that? (Reminder: There are 12 inches in a foot.)

When Glitter Meets Glue

When you do crafts, nothing jazzes up your artwork like glitter. A stripe of glue, a sprinkle of glitter on it, and suddenly your drawing is sparkling—along with your fingers, your nose, and your hair. You'll also get glitter on your clothes, which will fall to the carpet and sparkle for a good 2-3 years. Thousands of years ago cavemen made glitter by grinding up mica (a sparkly rock), but now glitter is actually zillions of tiny foil pieces. It's almost impossible to wipe up every last bit of glitter, and it seems like it sticks around forever. Good thing it's so pretty.

**Wee ones:** If you squirt 6 dots of glue and 2 wiggly lines, how many sparkly shapes will you get when you sprinkle the glitter?

**Little kids:** If you dump 8 pinches of glitter onto your glue-covered drawing, then shake off 4 pinches worth of it, how many pinches of glitter stay on your drawing?

**Big kids:** If you have 5 glitter specks on your hands, 10 in your hair, and 6 more on your face, how many specks are stuck to you?

**Bonus:** If a teaspoon of your favorite glitter has 200 specks, and you dump a tablespoon of that onto your art project, how many specks is that? (Reminder: A tablespoon equals 3 teaspoons.)

Bath Math

After a whole day of getting stuff on you—mud, sand, glitter, hot fudge—now you have to wash it all off. Soap is that magical stuff that grabs onto all kinds of dirt and muck, but also gets rinsed away by water. Showers use a lot less water—just 10-20 gallons, compared with 40 or even 50 for a bath. But with a bath you can sit and turn that soap into bubbles and suds. You can also have other things swimming around with you: boats, squirt toys, and maybe some live animals, too.

● **Wee ones:** That octopus is holding 4 "hands" up out of the tub (if you can call them hands). If 1 of those hands is holding soap, how many of the waving hands aren't?

●● **Little kids:** If you and your pet octopus take a bath, how many legs do you have altogether? (An octopus has 8 legs.)

●●● **Big kids:** If you run a bath of 30 gallons but manage to splash 5 gallons of water out of the tub, how much water is left to clean you off?

★ **Bonus:** If your bathtub holds 40 gallons, and you can let 2 seahorses swim around for every 8 gallons, how many seahorses can take a bath with you?

Answers: 3 "hands"; 10 legs; 25 gallons; 10 seahorses (2 for each of the 5 8-gallon sets).

There's No Wrong Time for Pajamas

At the end of a long, tiring day, it feels great to put on your fleecy pajamas, all cute and cuddly with stars, bunnies, and ninja warriors. Pajamas often have fun patterns and pictures, and they might actually be your favorite outfit. So why do we wear them only at night? Why save our most awesome clothes for when it's dark and you're hidden in bed? Maybe it's time we all tried wearing our pajamas out of the house to mix things up.

♥ **Wee ones:** If you always wear your same 3 pajama sets in the same order—blue, then stripes, then glow-in-the-dark, then blue, then stripes—which ones do you wear next?

♥♥ **Little kids:** If you have 6 pajama bottoms and 8 pajama tops, which pajama half is running low, and by how many?

♥♥♥ **Big kids:** If you sleep in your PJs from 8:00 p.m. until 7:00 a.m., then wear them to school for another 6 hours, how many hours do you get to wear them?

★ **Bonus:** If you wear your PJs for all but 6 hours of the day, and half of those PJ hours were in broad daylight, for how many daring hours did you wear your PJs in daylight?

Chapter 3

PERSONAL FAVORITES

85 59 3 125 18 6 0 56 238 73 50

Color Me _____

Maybe you should try dyeing your hair blue. Or your pet hamster's fur blue. Maybe you should make blue pancakes for breakfast. Anything can look great in blue, if blue's your favorite color. The purple lovers and periwinkle fans can do the same with their pancakes, too. By the way, you don't have to stick to plain, old rainbow tones like red or green for your favorite color. If you want your waffles to be frog-skin olive or chewing-gum-stuck-under-the-desk pink, go for it.

Wee ones: If some say the rainbow has 6 colors—red, orange, yellow, green, blue, and purple—while others add indigo as 1 more, how many colors does that "indigo" rainbow have?

Little kids: If you paint your bedroom and the kitchen neon orange (because you just love neon orange), and each room has 4 walls, how many walls did you paint?

Big kids: If you have 17 pet bunnies and you dye them your favorite shade of purple, how many purple bunny ears do they have?

Bonus: If you make 4 batches of 9 crocodile-green pancakes, and you need 1 drop of food coloring for every 3 pancakes, how many drops do you need?

Answers: 7 colors; 8 walls; 34 purple ears; 12 drops of food coloring.

Name Game

Chances are the best name you've ever heard is your own. It's your favorite name out there, and you've loved hearing people say it ever since you were born. Maybe you have a simple 3-part name, like Annabella Featherhat Frump. Or maybe you ended up with a 4-part name, like Francis Wigglewart Birdbaum Smith. You're going to have to sign your name many, many times during your life, so if you have a long name, you're going to have a lot of writing to do.

Wee ones: If Danger really is your middle name, how many letters is that?

Little kids: How many more letters does Annabella Featherhat Frump have in her middle name than her first name?

Big kids: If there's space to write 18 letters and your name is unfortunately 32 letters long, how many letters will get left off?

⭐ **Bonus:** If our buddy Francis over there just goes by Frank Smith, how many letters does he avoid writing?

Answers: 6 letters; 1 more letter; 14 letters; 20 letters (30 vs. 10).

Food Fest

Even though we all have the same kind of tongue, we don't all love the same foods. Your favorite might be cereal or fish sticks or string beans dipped in ketchup. But others may have different ideas. There's the messy crowd who thinks pizza, meatballs, caramel, and anything else sloppy tastes great. Then there's the mix-it-up crowd, who thinks food is yummiest when it has zillions of flavors mixed together. What's your favorite food and what's its strangest ingredient?

Wee ones: How many foods that you love can you count? Count as many as you can.

Little kids: If you could eat chocolate-dipped hot dogs for breakfast once a week, for lunch once a week, and for dinner 3 times a week, how many times would you eat them each week?

Big kids: If you could eat pineapple-mustard ice cream twice a day every day, how many times would you eat it in a week—and would you get sick of it? (Remember, a week has 7 days.)

Bonus: Which way do you get to eat more banana-applesauce pizza: 3 times a week for 4 weeks, or all the even days in a month?

Answers: 1, 2, 3 . . . practice counting; 5 times; 14 times; on the even days.

43

No Matter How You Slice It

Hey, when's your birthday? Each time that date comes around, you get to celebrate that you're one year older. But just adding another candle to your cake doesn't make a big-enough deal of it. Shouldn't we get to eat one more piece of cake in total every year? And how about your half birthday, which is that same-numbered day 6 months later—shouldn't we eat cake then, too? Hmmm . . . if we do the math right, we can get a heck of a lot more cake out of this birthday thing.

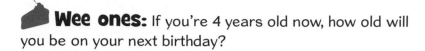 **Wee ones:** If you're 4 years old now, how old will you be on your next birthday?

Little kids: If you eat 4 pieces of cake on your 4th birthday and 5 on your 5th birthday, how many pieces did you snag in total?

Big kids: In what month do September birthdays have their half birthday?

Bonus: If you eat 1 piece of cake on your 1st birthday, 2 on your 2nd, and so on, how many pieces total have you eaten by your 10th birthday?

Answers: 5 years old; 9 pieces; March; 55 pieces, including that day.

45

It's a Zoo out There

In the whole big, smelly animal kingdom, you probably have a favorite animal. Or maybe a couple of favorites, because how can you decide between an octopus or a koala? They're so different, but they're both so cool. Really, picking a favorite animal is complicated. You have to decide between fur or feathers, slimy or scaly, weird-shaped snouts or weird-shaped tails. Then there's that smell problem, especially if your favorite happens to be the skunk. After figuring that all out, can you keep your favorite animal as a pet?

🐤 **Wee ones:** If you have a pet lizard because that's your favorite animal, how many shoes do you and he need altogether, assuming your lizard wants shoes? (Lizards have 4 feet.)

🐤🐤 **Little kids:** If your favorite animal is the squid (8 arms and 2 tentacles), and your friend's favorite is the ladybug (6 legs), how many skinny limbs do they have together?

🐤🐤🐤 **Big kids:** If you're sneaking ostrich chicks into your house because you want lots of pet ostriches, and you can fit 10 at a time through the window, how many batches of birds do you need to sneak in in order to bring in 63 chicks?

⭐ **Bonus:** If you and 5 friends each bring your favorite animal to a party, and half of you bring a zebra while half bring a peacock, how many friend and animal legs are in the group?

Snack Attack

As soon as someone came up with the idea of bite-sized, salty snacks—the chip, the cheese puff, the mini pretzel—we were all in trouble, because it's hard to eat just one. In some ways, it all started in 1853, when a grumpy customer complained about soggy French fries and the chef solved the problem by slicing them much thinner, thus accidentally inventing the potato chip. Whether your favorite snack is the potato chip, the mini pretzel, or the cute little crunchy goldfish, chances are you never eat just one.

Wee ones: If you're choosing between pretzels, potato chips, and nuts, how many snack choices do you have?

Little kids: If you're looking at 3 crunchy goldfish and they're looking back at you, how many fish eyes are looking at you? (Assume that even snack fish have 2 eyes apiece.)

Big kids: If a box of 36 snack packs has 10 goldfish packs and 10 potato chip packs, how many packs of other snacks are there?

⭐ **Bonus:** If a cup can hold 40 goldfish or 20 mini-pretzels, which way do you score more snack pieces, getting 3 cups of fish or 5 cups of pretzels?

Water Works

Okay, so most of us have a favorite animal, color, and food. It's time we all pick a favorite water-spraying gadget, too. You can squirt a fine stream of water from a bath toy, or a whole bunch of thin streams using a lawn sprinkler. Even better are those sprinklers that wiggle around so you have no idea where the water will aim next. If you want to get serious, you can blast a lot of water from a garden hose. Or maybe you want to send one solid burst by chucking a water balloon. Once you pick your favorite gadget, now you just have to choose your target.

💧 **Wee ones:** If you throw water balloons in repeating order and you've already hurled yellow, purple, blue, yellow again and then purple, what color balloon do you lob next?

💧💧 **Little kids:** If your lawn sprinkler has 10 little holes and you manage to plug 3 of them with your fingers, how many streams of water are still spraying you?

💧💧💧 **Big kids:** How much water can you spray on someone in 10 seconds with a 2-gallon-per-second garden hose?

⭐ **Bonus:** If your rubber ducky squirts 2 cups of water at a time at your friend, and your friend's water blaster shoots 5 cups at a time back at you, which squirts more, 6 rubber duckies or 2 blasters?

Chapter 4

PERSONAL
HABITS

AAACHOOOOOOOO

3 66 75 503 9 2 48 7 82 29 5

From Lapkins to Wrapkins

Back when cavepeople ate meals, they just dribbled food all over whatever bearskin they were wearing. Today, we do a little bit better than that—we use napkins. Napkins catch food that falls off our forks and spoons, and give us something to wipe our messy mouths. Even though it's a hassle to put your napkin in your lap every meal, it makes a lot more sense to do that than, say, tie it around your head or fold it into a paper airplane. Let's see what happens when we don't use our napkins as lapkins.

Wee ones: If you have 1 napkin in your lap and 1 tied around your head like a pirate bandanna, how many napkins do you have?

Little kids: If at a dinner for 70 people every 10th person is wearing a napkin like a hat, starting with guest #10, which people are wearing hats?

Big kids: If your dinner table is 8 feet long, and your napkin-folded-into-a-paper-airplane flies the length of the table plus another 24 feet, how far did your napkin fly?

★ **Bonus:** If at 6:35 p.m. you open your napkin, but you already spilled soup on your lap at 6:18 p.m., by how many minutes was your napkin too late?

Answers: 2 napkins; 10, 20, 30, 40, 50, 60, 70; 32 feet; 17 minutes. 55

Duck, Duck, Moose

In general, there aren't many times when it's polite to make animal sounds. Whistling like a lovely little bird isn't so bad, but snorting like a hippo or squawking like a chicken might not go over so well with other people—especially in school, at the dentist, or in the middle of someone's wedding. But it's tempting to practice animal noises because, if you get good at it, you can really start sounding like a hippo or chicken. Then you just have to figure out how to look like one.

🗨 **Wee ones:** If you've already quacked 7 times like a duck, what number will the next quack be?

🗨🗨 **Little kids:** If you make 2 squawks, then a snort, then repeat in that order, what's the 8th sound you make?

🗨🗨🗨 **Big kids:** If you say "Hi!" by heehawing twice like a donkey, how many times do you heehaw to say hi to 9 friends?

⭐ **Bonus:** If your best cock-a-doodle-doo takes 5 seconds, how many times can you crow during a 1-minute TV ad? (That's 60 seconds.)

The Last Straw

Straws are incredibly handy for mealtime. They zip your drink to your mouth without dripping anything on your face, and make it easier to sip super-hot and super-cold drinks. Of course, what can go up a straw can also come back down, like through an elephant's trunk, and that's when the problems start. It generally isn't a good idea to shoot stuff back out of a straw. Blowing bubbles in your drink, spraying milkshake at the ceiling—it's all a bad idea, as we'll see when we do the math.

7 Wee ones: How many full loop-de-loops does that crazy straw have?

77 Little kids: If you can slurp up a milkshake in 12 seconds but spray it back out in just 2 seconds, how many seconds faster can you spray it than slurp it?

777 Big kids: If you slide the damp tip of a straw wrapper back onto the straw and then blow, you can blast it through the air. If you get 6 of those to stick to the ceiling, 7 to the wall, and 8 to the window, how many did you fire off?

★ **Bonus:** If every 3rd person at the table has a red-striped straw instead of blue-striped straw, and every 4th person is blowing bubbles, what color straw is the 2nd bubble-blower using?

Dinner with a Twist

There are many ways to eat spaghetti. One is to put one end of the noodle in your mouth and slurp it in, the way an aardvark might. That splatters sauce everywhere, so it isn't the best method for us or for the aardvarks. Another way is to cut it up with your fork and knife. But the most fun way to eat spaghetti is to twirl it. Stick your fork into the spaghetti on your plate and give a twist, and the noodles will slowly wrap around into a nice, neat ball. But proper manners say to take only 3 strands at a time, or you'll get a giant blob that you'll end up, well, slurping.

Ⓔ Wee ones: If you twirl 3 strands of spaghetti on your fork while your cousin spins 5 strands, who has the bigger bite?

ⒺⒺ Little kids: If you have 8 strands of spaghetti on your plate and you twirl 3 on your fork, how many noodles are left on the plate?

ⒺⒺⒺ Big kids: If you bravely twirl 8 strands at a time, how many giant bites does it take to eat your plate of 72 noodles?

★ Bonus: What's the smallest bite size you need to finish 72 noodles in 20 bites?

Singing for Your Supper

We've been told that people aren't supposed to sing at the table. Why is that? Well, it isn't just because some people aren't great singers—who wants to listen to a bunch of screeching while trying to eat? It's also because maybe not everyone wants to sing the same song. If you've ever heard two songs play at the same time, you know how bad that can sound. Maybe that's why the only acceptable song to sing together is "Happy Birthday." Everyone knows the words and the tune.

♪ **Wee ones:** If at the table people are singing "Happy Birthday," "Old Macdonald," "Row Row Row Your Boat," and the alphabet song, how many songs are they singing?

♪♪ **Little kids:** If 10 friends sing "Happy Birthday" to you but only 1 person sings it right, how many are singing it wrong?

♪♪♪ **Big kids:** If during dinner you spend 25 minutes eating and another 14 minutes singing, how long does dinner drag on?

★ **Bonus:** If you eat for 16 minutes and sing for twice as long, now how long does dinner take?

Power-Sneezer

We don't sneeze on purpose, or at least most of us don't. Your body decides when and how to sneeze, based on whatever germs or dust you're trying to get out of your nose or mouth. Have you noticed that you can't keep your eyes open when you sneeze? That's because we sneeze at about 200 miles per hour, more than 3 times as fast as the cars on a highway. That's why you have to cover your mouth when you sneeze: not just to avoid spreading germs, but also to avoid knocking everybody over.

Wee ones: If you've already sneezed 6 times, what number sneeze comes next?

Little kids: If you're a real power-sneezer and in one blast you knock over 7 bushes, 6 bikes, and someone's dog, how many things did you knock over?

Big kids: If you sneeze at 200 miles an hour while driving at 70 miles an hour, how many miles an hour faster than the car was your sneeze?

Bonus: If you sneeze at 200 miles per hour, how fast will your sneeze reach a town 20 miles away? (Reminder: An hour has 60 minutes.)

Bedlam

You don't start the day without putting on clothes, right? So why should your bed? And you don't wear your pants, socks, and underwear wrapped around your head with nothing on the rest of you, right? No, you wear your clothes from head to foot, and so should your bed. That's why it's a good habit to make your bed every morning. Many people kick the sheets off while sleeping, or the pillows go flying, or the blanket forms a giant knot with 13 stuffed animals inside. So if you don't straighten up every day, after a while, your bed will become a disaster zone.

Wee ones: How many socks have been flung off the bed?

Little kids: If instead of making your bed you build a fort out of 5 pillows, 2 beanbag chairs, and 2 blankets for the roof, how many parts does your fort have?

Big kids: If you clean your room by stuffing things under the bed, and you can fit 50 objects under there but you've already stuffed in 30, how many more items can you hide?

Bonus: If 1/2 of your 48 stuffed animals disappear into your bed and 1/3 of those are bunny rabbits, how many bunnies have gone missing?

Snack Time for Fluffy

Just as we feed ourselves, we need to feed our pets, too. Your dog Josephine isn't as smart as you are, and your fish Henry is even less smart, and your cat Clawford isn't so smart either, no matter how much he pretends to be. These animal family members can't always figure out dinner for themselves. They're counting on *you*. So you have to get in the habit of feeding them the right amount of food at the right time— otherwise things can go haywire.

Wee ones: If you're counting out 1 treat for each of your 7 pet gerbils, what numbers do you need to count?

Little kids: If you forget to feed your pet rabbit Munchy, and she breaks into the bag of 10 carrots in the fridge, how many did she eat if you find only 2 left?

Big kids: If your underfed dog Murray gets loose in the kitchen and eats 9 burgers, 9 hot dogs, and 9 cookies, how many food items did Murray eat?

Bonus: If your dog eats twice as much as your cat, who eats twice as much as your hamster, how many biscuits do they devour altogether if the hamster eats 3?

Answers: 1. 2, 3, 4, 5, 6, 7; 8 carrots; 27 food items; 21 biscuits.

Tongue Twister

Can you click your tongue? Or wiggle your ears? Or make a popping sound by pulling your finger out of your mouth? One great thing about the human body is all the tricks you can do with it. You're like a walking musical instrument and battery-operated toy put together. If you're double-jointed, you can bend your fingers, arms, and maybe even your legs in all kinds of frightening ways and wow everyone on the playground. And if you can add some sound effects, all the better.

Wee ones: If you learn how to whistle, snap your fingers, and roll your tongue, how many tricks can you do?

Little kids: If among your 9 friends 6 of them can moonwalk, how many still need to learn?

Big kids: If you can whistle, snap, wiggle your ears, and tap-dance, how many ways can you perform 2 tricks at the same time?

Bonus: If a kid will give you a nickel to see you put your foot behind your head, how much can you earn from an audience of 22 kids?

Answers: 3 tricks; 3 friends; 6 combos (WS, WE, WT, SE, ST, ET): $1.10.

48 3 107 9 6 15 36 143 85 3 8 2

Chapter 5

PERSONAL BESTS

1 30 45 537 12 4 72 0 20 8 13

On the Run

It's funny we ever bother walking anywhere when we can get places so much faster by running. As a kid, chances are you can walk a full mile in an hour, but you might run closer to 4 or 5 miles an hour. And fast grown-ups can run about 12-15 miles per hour. Whether you're a kid or a grown-up, you tend to run fastest when you're racing against someone else—or when you're running from a lion or rhino that's chasing you. Luckily, you won't run into any of those animals on the playground.

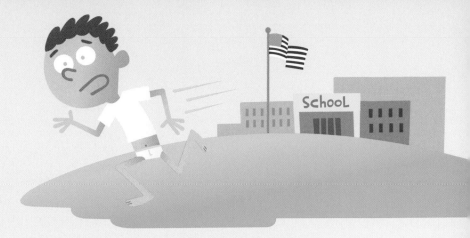

Wee ones: If you're running at 4 miles per hour and your friend's loose guinea pig is waddling at 3 miles per hour, can you catch the guinea pig?

Little kids: If you spot a rabbit in the yard and start chasing it at 5 miles an hour, but the bunny hops 7 miles an hour faster than you, how fast can that bunny hop?

Big kids: If you get to school and suddenly realize you totally forgot to put on pants, and you start running home at 8:22 a.m., when do you get home if it takes you 16 minutes?

★ Bonus: If your friend's dog is on the loose running 20 miles per hour, how many minutes will it take the dog to reach the park 1 mile away? (Reminder: An hour has 60 minutes.)

Answers: Yes!; 12 miles per hour; 8:38 a.m.; 3 minutes.

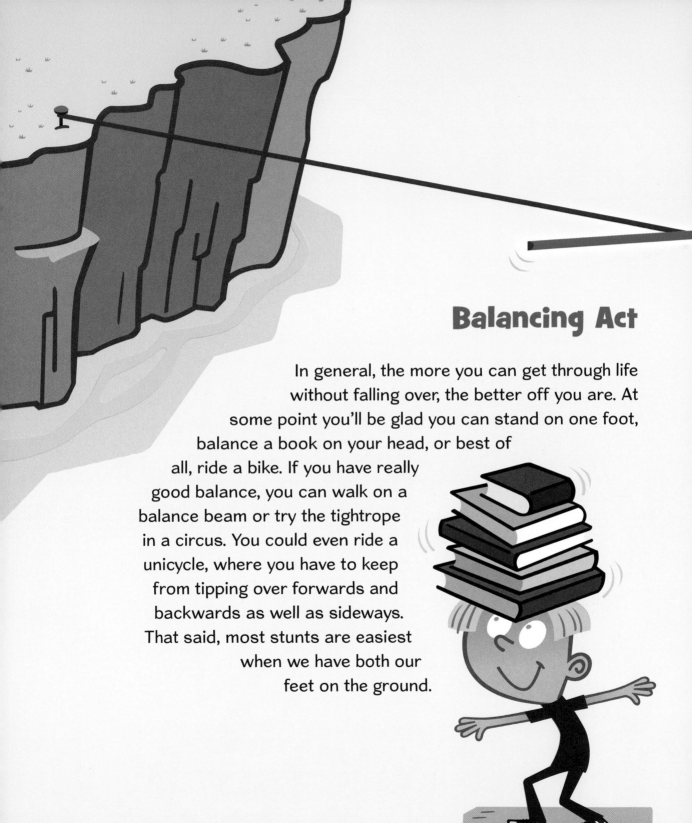

Balancing Act

In general, the more you can get through life without falling over, the better off you are. At some point you'll be glad you can stand on one foot, balance a book on your head, or best of all, ride a bike. If you have really good balance, you can walk on a balance beam or try the tightrope in a circus. You could even ride a unicycle, where you have to keep from tipping over forwards and backwards as well as sideways. That said, most stunts are easiest when we have both our feet on the ground.

Wee ones: If that guy is balancing 5 books on his head and that girl is balancing 1 bird, how many items are they balancing in total?

Little kids: If you try running with a watermelon on your head and it stays for 18 seconds, then your friend tries and balances it for 15 seconds, who balanced it longer?

Big kids: If your friend can balance while standing on your shoulders, and your friend is 52 inches tall and your shoulders are 40 inches off the ground, how high is the top of your friend's head?

Bonus: If you can ride your bike 39 feet without tipping over, but when you ride doubled up with your friend you make it only 1/3 as far, how far did the two of you ride?

Having a Ball

It's funny how so many sports and games use their own kind of ball, all in different shapes and sizes. Footballs, volleyballs, bouncy kick balls—they're all different. What's more, some of the smaller balls weigh more than the bigger ones. Sure, a Ping Pong ball weighs less than a baseball, but a little golf ball actually weighs more than a whiffle ball full of holes. A beach ball weighs almost nothing, but a much smaller bowling ball can weigh 20-30 pounds—a good chunk of what you weigh. For everyone's sake, don't throw one of those over the volleyball net.

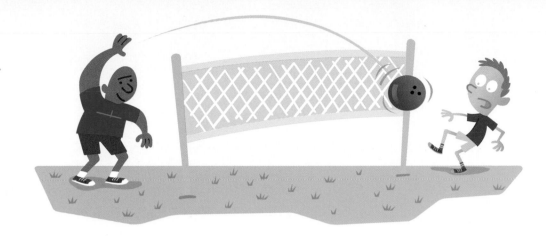

Wee ones: If a baseball weighs 5 ounces and a football weighs 14 ounces, which one weighs more?

Little kids: If you throw a rubber bouncy ball and it bounces a distance of 5 feet on each bounce, where does it hit on the 4th bounce?

Big kids: If you can kick a soccer ball 24 feet but a bowling ball only 3 feet (ouch!), how many kicks does it take to move the bowling ball 24 feet?

Bonus: If you can smack a tennis ball 29 feet, but can hit a baseball twice as far, and the house next door is 52 feet away, are you in danger of hitting it?

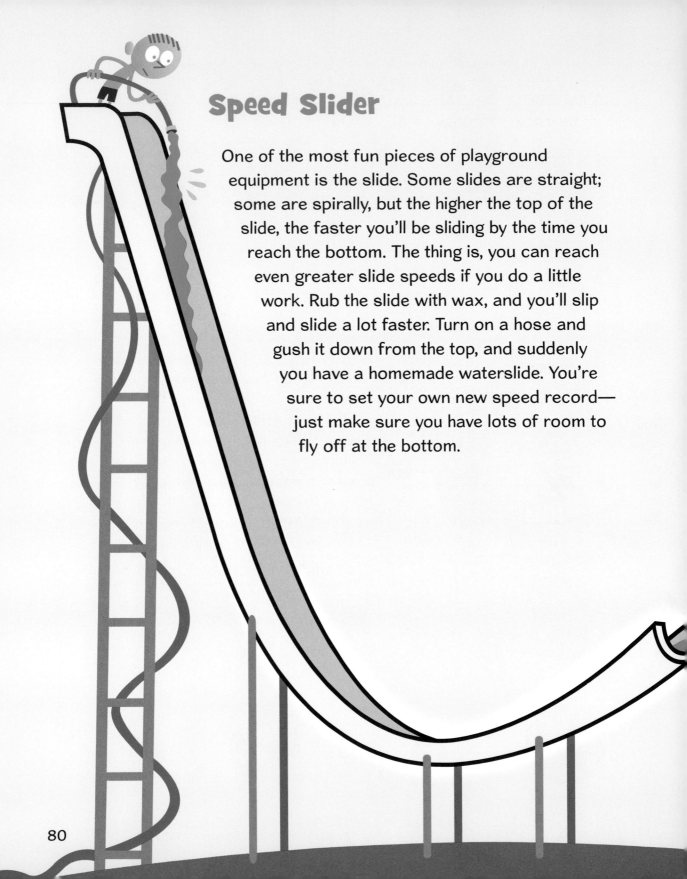

Speed Slider

One of the most fun pieces of playground equipment is the slide. Some slides are straight; some are spirally, but the higher the top of the slide, the faster you'll be sliding by the time you reach the bottom. The thing is, you can reach even greater slide speeds if you do a little work. Rub the slide with wax, and you'll slip and slide a lot faster. Turn on a hose and gush it down from the top, and suddenly you have a homemade waterslide. You're sure to set your own new speed record— just make sure you have lots of room to fly off at the bottom.

Wee ones: Which ride takes longer, a 13-second spiral slide or an 11-second straight slide?

Little kids: If it takes you 17 seconds to slide down a giant spiral slide, but when you turn it into a waterslide it takes a whole 10 seconds off your time, now how fast do you slide it?

Big kids: If you wax your slide with crayons (*after* getting permission) and start with a 24-crayon box, how many do you have left if you use up 16 crayons?

Bonus: If you can climb the big ladder in 20 seconds and then slide down in 1/4 that time, how long does the whole trip take?

Memory Game

Just as good balance can be a big help, so is a good memory. We're born knowing basically nothing, then slowly we learn a few words like *mama*, *papa*, and our own name, and by the time we're 4 years old we know almost 2,000 words. We also remember things that have happened to us, and songs we like, and the names of all the characters in our favorite show. They say elephants have a great memory, but let's see if you can match those guys.

Wee ones: If you're turning 5 years old and you can still remember your 3rd birthday party, for how long have you remembered it?

Little kids: Look at the number sequence 4 2 5 3 8 9. Now look away and see if you can say it, and say it again!

Big kids: If a song runs for 4 minutes at a pace of 40 words per minute, how many words (either new or repeating) do you have to remember to learn the song?

★ **Bonus:** . . . and can you still remember that string of numbers?

Through the Roof

Can you jump? And if you can, how high? Have you ever measured how high off the floor your feet can go? Jumping straight up in the air is a useful skill, after all, because for a second or two it makes you taller than you really are. In that moment, you can grab a balloon string before it floats away. You can do a high five with really tall people. You can reach snacks that your parents keep on high shelves where they think you can't reach them. It would be even better if we could fly, but jumping high counts for something.

🎈 **Wee ones:** If you jump 8 times while counting, what number jump comes next?

🎈🎈 **Little kids:** If you're 3 feet tall and your arm can reach 1 foot above you, and you can jump 2 feet high off the floor, how high can you reach at the peak of your jump?

🎈🎈🎈 **Big kids:** If you're 50 inches tall and stand on a 10-inch chair, and you can reach 20 inches above your head and jump 20 inches, can you touch your 8-foot-high ceiling? (Reminder: There are 12 inches in 1 foot.)

⭐ **Bonus:** That nursery rhyme says that the cow jumps over the moon, which is about 240,000 miles away. If a cow could jump 2 miles high, how many miles higher would it have to jump to clear the moon?

EQUATION CHART
THE MATH BEHIND THE FUN

Title	Wee ones	Little kids	Big kids	Bonus
Stick People	3>2	2+2=4	3x5=15	350-206=144
The Tooth of the Matter	1,2,3,4,5	5x2=10	9+3+7=19	38/2=19
Foot in Your Mouth—or on Your Arm	Arm longer than hand	5-2=3	41+2=43	7x7=49
You've Nailed It	1,2,3,4,5	5+5+5+5=20	4x10=40	(3x12)+7=43
Who's Faster, the Tortoise or the Hair?	6>4	2+2+2+2=8	26+11=37	28x2=56
Taste Test	1,2,3,4,5,6,7	34-(3x10)=4	3x8=24	4600/2=2300
Are We There Yet?	Rectangle	12-10=2	22-9=13	3:28 p.m.+45 min=4:13 p.m.
Getting Loud	6 comes after 5	1+6-3=4	A+BCDEFGABCD	92-75=17
Under Where?	Alternate striped and elephant	9+4=13	30-3-8=19	30-(7x4)=2
An Eye for an Eye	Triangles	Count by 10s to 100	72-51=21	365x2 =730
Socks on the Run	1,2,3,4,5,6,7,8,9,10	10-6=4	17-(6x2)=5	Combinatorials: 4 choose 2 permitting doubles
Mess Magnet	1,2,3	11>7	80-60=20	200+(2 x 200)+ (2 x 200)=1000
It's a Wrap	4>2	14,15,16,17	53+10=63	96/(12/4)=32
When Glitter Meets Glue	6+2=8	8-4=4	5+10+6=21	200x3=600
Bath Math	4-1=3	2+8=10	30-5=25	2x(40/8)=10
There's No Wrong Time for Pajamas	Blue-stripe-glow pattern	8-6=2	(8 p.m.→7 a.m.)+6 =17hrs	(24-6)/2=9
Color Me ___	6+1=7	4+4=8	17x2=34	(4x9)/3=12
Name Game	1,2,3,4,5,6	10-9=1	32-18=14	(7+10+8+5)- (5+5)=20
Food Fest	Count up from 1	1+1+3=5	2x7=14	3x4 < 30/2

Title	Wee ones	Little kids	Big kids	Bonus
No Matter How You Slice It	5 comes after 4	4+5=9	September+6 months	1+2+3+4+5+6+7+8+9+10=55
It's a Zoo out There	4+2=6	8+2+6=16	63 is 6 tens plus 3 ones	(5+1)x2+4x(5+1)/2+2x(5+1)/2=30
Snack Attack	1,2,3	2+2+2=6 (or) 3x2=6	36-10-10=16	3x40>5x20
Water Works	Yellow-purple-blue pattern	10-3=7	10x2=20	2x6>5x2
From Lapkins to Wrapkins	1+1=2	Count by 10s to 70	8+24=32	6:35 p.m.-6:18 p.m.=17min
Duck, Duck, Moose	8 comes after 7	Squawk squawk snort pattern	2x9=18	60/5=12
The Last Straw	Count 7 loops	12-2=10	6+7+8=21	(4x2) not divisible by 3
Dinner with a Twist	5>3	8-3=5	72/8=9	72<4 20s
Singing for Your Supper	1,2,3,4	10-1=9	25+14=39	16+(2x16)=48
Power-Sneezer	7 comes after 6	7+6+1=14	200-70=130	(20/200)x60=6
Bedlam	Count 6 socks in picture	5+2+2=9	50-30=20	(48/2)/3=8
Snack Time for Fluffy	Count to 7	10-2=8	9+9+9=27	3+(2x3)+(2x6)=21
Tongue Twister	1,2,3	9-6=3	Combinatorials: 4 choose 2	22x¢.05=$1.10
On the Run	4>3	7+5=12	8:22 a.m.+16min =8:38 a.m.	(1/20)x60=3
Balancing Act	5+1=6	18>15	52+40=92	39/3=13
Having a Ball	14>5	5+5+5+5=20	24/3=8	29x2>52
Speed Slider	13>11	17-10=7	24-16=8	20+(20/4)=25
Memory Game	5-3=2	remember a sequence of digits	40x4=160	recall the sequence again
Through the Roof	9 comes after 8	3+1+2=6	50+10+20+20= 100>96	240,000-2=239,998

Thank you for reading this Feiwel and Friends book.
The Friends who made

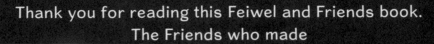

Bedtime Math²

possible are:

Jean Feiwel
publisher

Liz Szabla
editor in chief

Rich Deas
senior creative director

Holly West
associate editor

Dave Barrett
executive managing editor

Lauren A. Burniac
editor

Nicole Liebowitz Moulaison
production manager

Anna Roberto
assistant editor

Follow us on Facebook or visit us online at mackids.com.

OUR BOOKS ARE FRIENDS FOR LIFE